Old Age

and

Death

Jacques Casanova de Seingalt

[ZHINGOORA BOOKS]

OLD AGE AND DEATH OF CASANOVA

APPENDIX AND SUPPLEMENT

Whether the author died before the work was complete, whether the concluding volumes were destroyed by himself or his literary executors, or whether the MS. fell into bad hands, seems a matter of uncertainty, and the materials available towards a continuation of the Memoirs are extremely fragmentary. We know, however, that Casanova at last succeeded in obtaining his pardon from the authorities of the Republic, and he returned to Venice, where he exercised the honourable office of secret agent of the State Inquisitors—in plain language, he became a spy. It seems that the Knight of the Golden Spur made a rather indifferent "agent;" not surely, as a French writer suggests, because the dirty work was too dirty for his fingers, but probably because he was getting old and stupid and out-of-date, and failed to keep in touch with new forms of turpitude. He left Venice again and paid a visit to Vienna, saw beloved Paris once more, and there met Count Wallenstein, or Waldstein. The conversation turned on magic and the occult sciences, in, which Casanova was an adept, as the reader of the Memoirs will remember, and the count took a fancy to the charlatan. In short Casanova became librarian at the count's Castle of Dux, near Teplitz, and there he spent the fourteen remaining years of his life.

As the Prince de Ligne (from whose Memoirs we learn these particulars) remarks, Casanova's life had been a stormy and adventurous one, and it might have been expected that he would have found his patron's library a pleasant refuge after so many toils and travels. But the man carried rough weather and storm in his own heart, and found daily opportunities of mortification and resentment. The coffee was ill made, the maccaroni not cooked in the true Italian style, the dogs had bayed during the night, he had been made to dine at a small table, the parish priest had tried to convert him, the soup had been served too hot on purpose to annoy him, he had not been introduced to a distinguished guest, the count had lent a book without telling him, a groom had not taken off his hat; such were his complaints. The fact is Casanova felt his dependent position and his utter poverty, and was all the more determined to stand to his dignity as a man who had talked with all the crowned heads of Europe, and had fought a duel with the Polish general. And he had another reason for finding life bitter— he had lived beyond his time. Louis XV. was dead, and Louis XVI. had been guillotined; the Revolution had come; and Casanova, his dress, and his manners, appeared as odd and antique as some "blood of the Regency" would appear to us of these days. Sixty years before, Marcel, the famous dancing-master, had taught young Casanova how to enter a room with a lowly and ceremonious bow; and still, though the eighteenth century is drawing to a close, old Casanova enters the rooms of Dux with the same stately bow, but now everyone laughs. Old Casanova treads the grave measures of the minuet; they applauded his dancing once, but now everyone laughs. Young Casanova was always dressed in the height of the fashion; but the age of powder, wigs, velvets, and silks has departed, and old Casanova's attempts at elegance ("Strass" diamonds have replaced the genuine stones with him) are likewise greeted with laughter. No wonder the old adventurer denounces the whole house of Jacobins and canaille; the world, he feels, is permanently out of joint for him; everything is cross, and everyone is in a conspiracy to drive the iron into his soul.

At last these persecutions, real or imaginary, drive him away from Dux; he considers his genius bids him go, and, as before, he obeys. Casanova has but little pleasure or profit out of this his last journey; he has to dance attendance in ante-chambers; no one will give him any office, whether as tutor, librarian, or chamberlain. In one quarter only is he well received—namely, by the famous Duke of Weimar; but in a few days he becomes madly jealous of the duke's more famous proteges, Goethe and Wieland, and goes off declaiming against them and German literature generally—with which literature he was wholly unacquainted. From Weimar to Berlin; where there are Jews to whom he has introductions. Casanova thinks them ignorant, superstitious, and knavish; but they lend him money, and he gives bills on Count Wallenstein, which are paid. In six weeks the wanderer returns to Dux, and is welcomed with open arms; his journeys are over at last.

But not his troubles. A week after his return there are strawberries at dessert; everyone is served before himself, and when the plate comes round to him, it is empty. Worse still: his portrait is missing from his room, and is discovered 'salement placarde a la porte des lieux d'aisance'!

Five more years of life remained to him. They were passed in such petty mortifications as we have narrated, in grieving over his 'afreuse vieillesse', and in laments over the conquest of his native land Venice, once so splendid and powerful. His appetite began to fail, and with it failed his last source of pleasure, so death came to him somewhat as a release. He received the sacraments with devotion, exclaimed,—

"Grand Dieu, et vous tous temoins de ma mort, j'ai vecu en philosophe, et je meurs en Chretien," and so died.

It was a quiet ending to a wonderfully brilliant and entirely useless career. It has been suggested that if the age in which Casanova lived had been less corrupt, he himself might have used his all but universal talents to some advantage, but to our mind Casanova would always have remained Casanova. He came of a family of adventurers, and the reader of his Memoirs will remark how he continually ruined his prospects by his ineradicable love for disreputable company. His "Bohemianism" was in his blood, and in his old age he regrets—not his past follies, but his inability to commit folly any longer. Now and again we are inclined to pronounce Casanova to be an amiable man; and if to his generosity and good nature he had added some elementary knowledge of the distinction between right and wrong, he might certainly have laid some claim to the character. The Prince de Ligne draws the following portrait of him under the name of Aventuros:

"He would be a handsome man if he were not ugly; he is tall and strongly built, but his dark complexion and his glittering eyes give him a fierce expression. He is easier to annoy than amuse; he laughs little but makes others laugh by the peculiar turn he gives to his conversation. He knows everything except those matters on the knowledge of which he chiefly prides himself, namely, dancing, the French language, good taste, and knowledge of the world. Everything about him is comic, except his comedies; and all his writings are philosophical, saving those which treat of philosophy. He is a perfect well of knowledge, but he quotes Homer and Horace ad nauseam."

SUPPLEMENT TO

THE MEMOIRS OF
JACQUES CASANOVA
DE SEINGALT
Containing an Outline of Casanova's career from the
year 1774, when his own Memoirs abruptly
end, until his death in 1798

PART THE FIRST

VENICE 1774-1782 CASANOVA'S RETURN TO VENICE

Thus Casanova ended his Memoirs, concluding his narrative with his sojourn at Trieste, in January 1774, where he had remained, except for a few excursions, since the 15th November 1772. He was forty-nine years of age. Since his unfortunate experiences in England, the loss of his fortune and the failure of his efforts to obtain congenial and remunerative employment in Germany or Russia, he had come to concentrate his efforts on a return to his native city.

Of his faithful friends, the nobles Bragadin, Barbaro and Dandolo, the first had died in 1767, having gone into debt "that I might have enough," sending Casanova, from his death-bed, a last gift of a thousand crowns. Barbaro who had died also, in 1771, left Casanova a life-income of six sequins a month. The survivor, Dandolo, was poor, but until his death, he also gave Casanova a monthly provision of six sequins. However, Casanova was not without influential friends who might not only obtain a pardon from the State Inquisitors but also assist him to employment; and, in fact, it was through such influence as that wielded by the Avogador Zaguri and the Procurator Morosini, that Casanova received his pardon, and later, a position as "Confidant," or Secret Agent, to the Inquisitors at Venice.

Casanova re-entered Venice the 14th September 1774 and, presenting himself, on the 18th, to Marc-Antoine Businello, Secretary of the Tribunal of the Inquisitors of State, was advised that mercy had been accorded him by reason of his refutation of the History of the Venetian Government by Amelot de la Houssaie which he had written during his forty-two day imprisonment at Barcelona in 1768. The three Inquisitors, Francesco Grimani, Francesco Sagredo and Paolo Bembo, invited him to dinner to hear his story of his escape from The Leads.

In 1772, Bandiera, the Republic's resident at Ancona, drew this portrait of Casanova:

"One sees everywhere this unhappy rebel against the justice of the August Council, presenting himself boldly, his head carried high, and well equipped. He is received in many houses and announces his intention of going to Trieste and, from there, of returning to Germany. He is a man of forty years or more," [in reality, forty-seven] "of high stature and excellent appearance, vigorous, of a very brown color, the eye bright, the wig short and chestnut-brown. He is said to be haughty and disdainful; he speaks at length, with spirit and erudition." [Letter of information to the Very Illustrious Giovanni Zon, Secretary of the August Council of Ten at Venice. 2 October 1772.]

Returning to Venice after an absence of eighteen years, Casanova renewed his acquaintance with many old friends, among whom were:

The Christine of the Memoirs. Charles, who married Christine, the marriage being arranged by Casanova while in Venice in 1747, was of financial assistance to Casanova, who "found him a true friend." Charles died "a few months before my last departure from Venice," in 1783.

Mlle. X—— C—— V——, really Giustina de Wynne, widow of the Count Rosenberg, Austrian Ambassador at Venice. "Fifteen years afterwards, I saw her again and she was a widow, happy enough, apparently, and enjoying a great reputation on account of her rank, wit and social qualities, but our connection was never renewed."

Callimena, who was kind to him "for love's sake alone" at Sorrento in 1770.

Marcoline, the girl he took away from his younger brother, the Abby Casanova, at Geneva in 1763.

Father Balbi, the companion of his flight from The Leads.

Doctor Gozzi, his former teacher at Padua, now become Arch-Priest of St. George of the Valley, and his sister Betting. "When I went to pay him a visit . . . she breathed her last in my arms, in 1776, twenty-four hours after my arrival. I will speak of her death in due time."

Angela Toselli, his first passion. In 1758 this girl married the advocate
Francesco Barnaba Rizzotti, and in the following year she gave birth to a
daughter, Maria Rizzotti (later married to a M. Kaiser) who lived at
Vienna and whose letters to Casanova were preserved at Dux.

C—— C——, the young girl whose love affair with Casanova became involved with that of the nun M—— M—— Casanova found her in Venice "a widow and poorly off."

The dancing girl Binetti, who assisted Casanova in his flight from Stuttgart in 1760, whom he met again in London in 1763, and who was the cause of his duel with Count Branicki at Warsaw in 1766. She danced frequently at Venice between 1769 and 1780.

The good and indulgent Mme. Manzoni, "of whom I shall have to speak very often."

The patricians Andrea Memmo and his brother Bernardo who, with P. Zaguri were personages of considerable standing in the Republic and who remained his constant friends. Andrea Memmo was the cause of the embarrassment in which Mlle. X—— C—— V—— found herself in Paris and which Casanova vainly endeavored to remove by applications of his astonishing specific, the 'aroph of Paracelsus'.

It was at the house of these friends that Casanova became acquainted with the poet, Lorenzo Da Ponte. "I made his acquaintance," says the latter, in his own Memoirs, "at the house of Zaguri and the house of Memmo, who both sought after his always interesting conversation, accepting from this man all he had of good, and closing their eyes, on account of his genius, upon the perverse parts of his nature."

Lorenzo Da Ponte, known above all as Mozart's librettist, and whose youth much resembled that of Casanova, was accused of having eaten ham on Friday and was obliged to flee from Venice in 1777, to escape the punishment of the Tribunal of Blasphemies. In his Memoirs, he speaks unsparingly of his compatriot and yet, as M. Rava notes, in the numerous letters he wrote Casanova, and which were preserved at Dux, he proclaims his friendship and admiration.

Irene Rinaldi, whom he met again at Padua in 1777, with her daughter who "had become a charming girl; and our acquaintance was renewed in the tenderest manner."

The ballet-girl Adelaide, daughter of Mme. Soavi, who was also a dancer, and of a M. de Marigny.

Barbara, who attracted Casanova's attention at Trieste, in 1773, while he was frequenting a family named Leo, but toward whom he had maintained an attitude of respect. This girl, on meeting him again in 1777, declared that "she had guessed my real feelings and had been amused by my foolish restraint."

At Pesaro, the Jewess Leah, with whom he had the most singular experiences at Ancona in 1772.

RELATIONS WITH THE INQUISITORS

Soon after reaching Venice, Casanova learned that the Landgrave of Hesse Cassel, following the example of other German princes, wished a Venetian correspondent for his private affairs. Through some influence he believed he might obtain this small employment; but before applying for the position he applied to the Secretary of the Tribunal for permission. Apparently nothing came of this, and Casanova obtained no definite employment until 1776.

Early in 1776, Casanova entered the service of the Tribunal of Inquisitors as an "occasional Confidant," under the fictitious name of
Antonio Pratiloni, giving his address as "at the Casino of S. E. Marco Dandolo."

In October 1780, his appointment was more definitely established and he was given a salary of fifteen ducats a month. This, with the six sequins of life-income left by Barbaro and the six given by Dandolo, gave him a monthly income of three hundred and eighty-four lires—about seventy-four U. S. dollars—from 1780 until his break with the Tribunal at the end of 1781.

In the Archives of Venice are preserved forty-eight letters from Casanova, including the Reports he wrote as a "Confidant," all in the same handwriting as the manuscript of the Memoirs. The Reports may be divided into two classes: those referring to commercial or industrial matters, and those referring to the public morals.

Among those of the first class, we find:

A Report relating to Casanova's success in having a change made in the route of the weekly diligence running from Trieste to Mestre, for which service, rendered during Casanova's residence at Trieste in 1773, he received encouragement and the sum of one hundred ducats from the Tribunal.

A Report, the 8th September 1776, with information concerning the rumored project of the future Emperor of Austria to invade Dalmatia after the death of Maria Theresa. Casanova stated he had received this information from a Frenchman, M. Salz de Chalabre, whom he had known in Paris twenty years before. This M. Chalabre [printed Calabre] was the pretended nephew of Mme. Amelin. "This young man was as like her as two drops of water, but she did not find that a sufficient reason for avowing herself his mother." The boy was, in fact, the son of Mme. Amelin and of M. de Chalabre, who had lived together for a long time.

A Report, the 12th of December 1776, of a secret mission to Trieste, in regard to a project of the court of Vienna for making Fiume a French port; the object being to facilitate communications between this port and the interior of Hungary. For this inquiry, Casanova received sixteen hundred lires, his expenditures amounting to seven hundred and sixty-six lires.

A Report, May-July 1779, of an excursion in the market of Ancona for information concerning the commercial relations of the Pontifical States with the Republic of Venice. At Forlì, in the course of this excursion, Casanova visited the dancing-girl Binetti. For this mission Casanova received forty-eight sequins.

A Report, January 1780, remarking a clandestine recruiting carried out by a certain Marrazzani for the [Prussian] regiment of Zarembal.

A Report, the 11th October 1781, regarding a so-called Baldassare Rossetti, a Venetian subject living at Trieste, whose activities and projects were of a nature to prejudice the commerce and industry of the Republic.

Among the Reports relating to public morals may be noted:

December 1776. A Report on the seditious character of a ballet called "Coriolanus." The back of this report is inscribed: "The impressario of S. Benedetto, Mickel de l'Agata, shall be summoned immediately; it has been ordered that he cease, under penalty of his life, from giving the ballet Coriolanus at the theater. Further, he is to collect and deposit all the printed programmes of this ballet."

December 1780. A Report calling to the attention of the Tribunal the scandalous disorders produced in the theaters when the lights were extinguished.

3rd May 1781. A Report remarking that the Abbe Carlo Grimani believed himself exempt, in his position as a priest, from the interdiction laid on patricians against frequenting foreign ministers and their suites. On the back of this Report is written:

"Ser Jean Carlo, Abbe Grimani, to be gently reminded, by the Secretary, of the injunction to abstain from all commerce with foreign ministers and their adherents."

Venetian nobles were forbidden under penalty of death from holding any communication with foreign ambassadors or their households. This was intended as a precaution to preserve the secrets of the Senate.

26th November 1781. A Report concerning a painting academy where nude studies were made, from models of both sexes, while scholars only twelve or thirteen years of age were admitted, and where dilettantes who were neither painters nor designers, attended the sessions.

22nd December 1781. By order, Casanova reported to the Tribunal a list of the principal licentious or antireligious books to be found in the libraries and private collections at Venice: la Pucelle; la Philosophie de l'Histoire; L'Esprit d'Helvetius; la Sainte Chandelle d'Arras; les Bijoux indiscrets; le Portier des Chartreux; les Posies de Baffo; Ode a Priape; de Piron; etc., etc.

In considering this Report, which has been the subject of violent criticism, we should bear in mind three points.

first—the Inquisitors required this information; second—no one in their employ could have been in a better position to give it than Casanova; third—Casanova was morally and economically bound, as an employee of the Tribunal, to furnish the information ordered, whatever his personal distaste for the undertaking may have been. We may even assume that he permitted himself to express his feelings in some indiscreet way, and his break with the Tribunal followed, for, at the end of 1781, his commission was withdrawn. Certainly, Casanova's almost absolute dependence on his salary, influenced the letter he wrote the Inquisitors at this time.

"To the Illustrious and Most Excellent Lords, the Inquisitors of State:

"Filled with confusion, overwhelmed with sorrow and repentance, recognizing myself absolutely unworthy of addressing my vile letter to Your Excellencies confessing that I have failed in my duty in the opportunities which presented themselves, I, Jacques Casanova, invoke, on my knees, the mercy of the Prince; I beg that, in compassion and grace, there may be accorded me that which, in all justice and on reflection, may be refused me.

"I ask the Sovereign Munificence to come to my aid, so that, with the means of subsistence, I may apply myself vigorously, in the future, to the service to which I have been privileged.

"After this respectful supplication, the wisdom of Your Excellencies may judge the disposition of my spirit and of my intentions."

The Inquisitors decided to award Casanova one month's pay, but specified that thereafter he would receive salary only when he rendered important services.

In 1782 Casanova made a few more Reports to the Tribunal, for one of which, regarding the failure of an insurance and commercial house at Trieste, he received six sequins. But the part of a guardian of the public morals, even through necessity, was undoubtedly unpleasant to him; and, in spite of the financial loss, it may be that his release was a relief.

III

FRANCESCA BUSCHINI

Intimately connected with Casanova's life at this period was a girl named Francesca Buschini. This name does not appear in any of the literary, artistic or theatrical records of the period, and, of the girl, nothing is known other than that which she herself tells us in her letters to Casanova. From these very human letters, however, we may obtain, not only certain facts, but also, a very excellent idea of her character. Thirty-two of her letters, dated between July 1779 and October 1787, written in the Venetian dialect, were preserved in the library at Dux.

She was a seamstress, although often without work, and had a brother, a younger sister and also a mother living with her. The probabilities are that she was a girl of the most usual sort, but greatly attached to Casanova who, even in his poverty, must have dazzled her as a being from another world. She was his last Venetian love, and remained a faithful correspondent until 1787; and it is chiefly from her letters, in which she comments on news contained in Casanova's letters to her, that light is thrown on the Vienna-Paris period, particularly, of Casanova's life. For this, Francesca has placed us greatly in her debt.

With this girl, at least between 1779 and 1782, Casanova rented a small house at Barbaria delle Tole, near S. Giustina, from the noble Pesaro at S. Stae. Casanova, always in demand for his wit and learning, often took dinner in the city. He knew that a place always awaited him at the house of Memmo and at that of

Zaguri and that, at the table of these patricians, who were distinguished by their intellectual superiority, he would meet men notable in science and letters. Being so long and so closely connected with theatrical circles, he was often seen at the theater, with Francesca. Thus, the 9th August 1786, the poor girl, in an excess of chagrin writes: "Where are all the pleasures which formerly you procured me? Where are the theatres, the comedies which we once saw together?"

On the 28th July 1779, Francesca wrote:

"Dearest and best beloved,

" . . . In the way of novelties, I find nothing except that S. E. Pietro Zaguri has arrived at Venice; his servant has been twice to ask for you, and I have said you were still at the Baths of Abano . . ."

The Casanova-Buschini establishment kept up relations, more or less frequent and intimate, with a few persons, most of whom are mentioned in Francesca's letters; the Signora Anzoletta Rizzotti; the Signora Elisabeth Catrolli, an ancient comedienne; the Signora Bepa Pezzana; the Signora Zenobia de Monti, possibly the mother of that Carlo de Monti, Venetian Consul at Trieste, who was a friend to Casanova and certainly contributed toward obtaining his pardon from the Inquisitors; a M. Lunel, master of languages, and his wife.

IV

PUBLICATIONS

Casanova's principal writings during this period were:

His translation of the Iliad, the first volume of which was issued in 1775, the second in 1777 and the third in 1778.

During his stay at Abano in 1778, he wrote the Scrutinio del libro, eulogies of M. de Voltaire "by various hands." In the dedication of this book, to the Doge Renier, he wrote, "This little book has recently come from my inexperienced pen, in the hours of leisure which are frequent at Abano for those who do not come only for the baths."

From January until July 1780, he published, anonymously, a series of miscellaneous small works, seven pamphlets of about one hundred pages each, distributed at irregular intervals to subscribers.

From the 7th October to the end of December, 1780, on the occasions of
the representations given by a troupe of French comedians at the San Angelo theater, Casanova wrote a little paper called The Messenger of Thalia. In one of the numbers, he wrote:

"French is not my tongue; I make no pretentions and, wrong or astray, I place on the paper what heaven sends from my pen. I give birth to phrases turned to Italian, either to see what they look like or to produce a style, and often, also, to draw, into a purist's snare, some critical doctor who does not know my humor or how my offense amuses me."

The "little romance" referred to in the following letter to "Mlle. X—— C—— V——," appeared in 1782, with the title; 'Di anecdoti vinizani militari a amorosi del secolo decimo quarto sotto i dogati di Giovanni Gradenigoe di Giovanni Dolfin'. Venezia, 1782.

V MLLE. X . . . C . . . V . . .

In 1782, a letter written by this lady, Giustina de Wynne, referring to a visit to Venice of Paul I, Grand Duke, afterward Emperor of Russia, and his wife, was published under the title of Du séjour des Comptes du Nord a Venise en janvier mdcclxxxii. If he had not previously done so, Casanova took this occasion to recall himself to the memory of this lady to whom he had once been of such great service. And two very polite letters were exchanged:

"Madam,

"The fine epistle which V. E. has allowed to be printed upon the sojourn of C. and of the C. du Nord in this city, exposes you, in the position of an author, to endure the compliments of all those who trouble themselves to write. But I flatter myself, Madam, that V. E. will not disdain mine.

"The little romance, Madam, a translation from my dull and rigid pen, is not a gift but a very paltry offering which I dare make to the superiority of your merit.

"I have found, Madam, in your letter, the simple, flowing style of gentility, the one which alone a woman of condition who writes to her friend may use with dignity. Your digressions and your thoughts are flowers which . . . (forgive an author who pilfers from you the delicious nonchalance of an amiable writer) or . . . a will-o'-the-wisp which, from time to time, issues from the work, in spite of the author, and burns the paper.

"I aspire, Madam, to render myself favorable to the deity to which reason advises me to make homage. Accept then the offering and render happy he who makes it with your indulgence.

"I have the honor to sign myself, if you will kindly permit me, with very profound respect.

"Giacomo Casanova."

"Monsieur

"I am very sensible, Monsieur, of the distinction which comes to me from your approbation of my little pamphlet. The interest of the moment, its references and the exaltation of spirits have gained for it the tolerance and favorable welcome of the good Venetians. It is to your politeness in particular, Monsieur, that I believe is due the marked success which my work has had with you. I thank you for the book which you sent me and I will risk thanking you in advance for the pleasure it will give me. Be persuaded of my esteem for yourself and for your talents. And I have the honor to be, Monsieur.

"Your very humble servant de Wynne de Rosemberg."

Among Casanova's papers at Dux was a page headed "Souvenir," dated the 2nd September 1791, and beginning: "While descending the staircase, the Prince de Rosemberg told me that Madame de Rosemberg was dead . . . .
This Prince de Rosemberg was the nephew of Giustina."

Giustina died, after a long illness, at Padua, the 21st August 1791, at the age of fifty-four years and seven months.

VI

LAST DAYS AT VENICE

Toward the end of 1782, doubtless convinced that he could expect nothing more from the Tribunal, Casanova entered the service of the Marquis Spinola as a secretary. Some years before, a certain Carletti, an officer in the service of the court of Turin, had won from the Marquis a wager of two hundred and fifty sequins. The existence of this debt seemed to have completely disappeared from the memory of the loser. By means of the firm promise of a pecuniary recompense, Casanova intervened to obtain from his patron a written acknowledgment of the debt owing to Carletti. His effort was successful; but instead of clinking cash, Carletti contented himself with remitting to the negotiator an assignment on the amount of the credit. Casanova's anger caused a violent dispute, in the course of which Carlo Grimani, at whose house the scene took place, placed him in the wrong and imposed silence.

The irascible Giacomo conceived a quick resentment. To discharge his bile, he found nothing less than to publish in the course of the month of August, under the title of: 'Ne amori ne donne ovvero la Stalla d'Angia repulita', a libel in which Jean Carlo Grimani, Carletti, and other notable persons were outraged under transparent mythological pseudonyms.

This writing embroiled the author with the entire body of the Venetian nobility.

To allow the indignation against him to quiet down, Casanova went to pass some days at Trieste, then returned to Venice to put his affairs in order. The idea of recommencing his wandering life alarmed him. "I have lived fifty-eight years," he wrote, "I could not go on foot with winter at hand, and when I think of starting on the road to resume my adventurous life, I laugh at myself in the mirror."

PART THE SECOND VIENNA-PARIS

I

1783-1785

TRAVELS IN 1783

Casanova left Venice in January 1783, and went to Vienna.

On the 16th April Elisabeth Catrolli wrote to him at Vienna:

"Dearest of friends,

"Your letter has given me great pleasure. Be assured, I infinitely regret your departure. I have but two sincere friends, yourself and Camerani. I do not hope for more. I could be happy if I could have at least one of you near me to whom I could confide my cruel anxieties.

"To-day, I received from Camerani a letter informing me that, in a former one, he had sent me a bill of exchange: I did not receive it, and I fear it has been lost.

"Dear friend, when you reach Paris, clasp him to your heart for me . . . In regard to Chechina [Francesca Buschini] I would say that I have not seen her since the day I took her your letter. Her mother is the ruin of that poor girl; let that suffice; I will say no more . . . . "

After leaving Venice, Casanova apparently took an opportunity to pay his last disrespects to the Tribunal. At least, in May 1783, M. Schlick, French Secretary at Venice, wrote to Count Vergennes: "Last week there reached the State Inquisitors an anonymous letter stating that, on the 25th of this month, an earthquake, more terrible than that of Messina, would raze Venice to the ground. This letter has caused a panic here. Many patricians have left the capital and others will follow their example. The author of the anonymous letter . . . is a certain Casanova, who wrote from Vienna and found means to slip it into the Ambassador's own mails."

In about four months, Casanova was again on the way to Italy. He paused for a week at Udine and arrived at Venice on the 16th June. Without leaving his barge, he paused at his house just long enough to salute Francesca. He left Mestre on Tuesday the 24th June and on the same day dined at the house of F. Zanuzzi at Bassano. On the 25th he left Bassano by post and arrived in the evening at Borgo di Valsugano.

On the 29th, he wrote to Francesca from the Augsbourg. He had stopped at Innsbruck to attend the theater and was in perfect health. He had reached Frankfort in forty-eight hours, traveling eighteen posts without stopping.

From Aix-la-Chapelle, on the 16th July, he wrote Francesca that he had met, in that city, Cattina, the wife of Pocchini. Pocchini was sick and in deep misery. Casanova, recalling all the abominable tricks this rogue had played on him refused Cattina the assistance she begged for in tears, laughed in her face, and said: "Farewell, I wish you a pleasant death."

At Mayence, Casanova embarked on the Rhine in company with the Marquis Durazzo, former Austrian Ambassador at Venice.

The voyage was excellent and in two days he arrived at Cologne, in rugged health, sleeping well and eating like a wolf.

On the 30th July he wrote to Francesca from Spa and in this letter enclosed a good coin. Everything was dear at Spa; his room cost eight lires a day with everything else in proportion.

On the 6th September he wrote from Antwerp to one of his good friends, the Abbe Eusebio della Lena, telling him that at Spa an English woman who had a passion for speaking Latin wished to submit him to trials which he judged it unnecessary to state precisely. He refused all her proposals, saying, however, that he would not reveal them to anyone; but that he did not feel he should refuse also "an order on her banker for twenty-five guineas."

On the 9th he wrote to Francesca from Brussels, and on the 12th he sent her a bill of exchange on the banker Corrado for one hundred and fifty lires. He said he had been intoxicated "because his reputation had required it." "This greatly astonishes me," Francesca responded, "for I have never seen you intoxicated nor even illuminated . . . . I am very happy that the wine drove away the inflammation in your teeth."

Practically all information of Casanova's movements in 1783 and 1784 is obtained from Francesca's letters which were in the library at Dux.

In her letters of the 27th June and 11th July, Francesca wrote Casanova that she had directed the Jew Abraham to sell Casanova's satin habit and velvet breeches, but could not hope for more than fifty lires because they were patched. Abraham had observed that at one time the habit had been placed in pledge with him by Casanova for three sequins.

On the 6th September, she wrote:

"With great pleasure, I reply to the three dear letters which you wrote me from Spa: the first of the 6th August, from which I learned that your departure had been delayed for some days to wait for someone who was to arrive in that city. I was happy that your appetite had returned, because good cheer is your greatest pleasure . . . .

"In your second letter which you wrote me from Spa on the 16th August, I noted with sorrow that your affairs were not going as you wished. But console yourself, dear friend, for happiness will come after trouble; at least, I wish it so, also, for you yourself can imagine in what need I find myself, I and all my family . . . . I have no work, because I have not the courage to ask it of anyone. My mother has not earned even enough to pay for the gold thread with the little cross which you know I love. Necessity made me sell it.

"I received your last letter of the 20th August from Spa with another letter for S. E. the Procurator Morosini. You directed me to take it to him myself, and on Sunday the last day of August, I did not fail to go there exactly at three o'clock. At once on my arrival, I spoke to a servant who admitted me without delay; but, my dear friend, I regret having to send you an unpleasant message. As soon as I handed him the letter, and before he even opened it, he said to me, 'I always know Casanova's affairs which trouble me.' After having read hardly more than a page, he said: 'I know not what to do!' I told him that, on the 6th of this month, I was to write you at Paris and that, if he would do me the honor of giving me his reply, I would put it in my letter. Imagine what answer he gave me! I was much surprised! He told me that I should wish you happiness but that he would not write to you again. He said no more. I kissed his hands and left. He did not give me even a sou. That is all he said to me . . . .

"S. E. Pietro Zaguri sent to me to ask if I knew where you were, because he had written two letters to Spa and had received no reply . . . ."

II

PARIS

On the night of the 18th or 19th September 1783, Casanova arrived at Paris.

On the 30th he wrote Francesca that he had been well received by his sister-in-law and by his brother, Francesco Casanova, the painter. Nearly all his friends had departed for the other world, and he would now have to make new ones, which would be difficult as he was no longer pleasing to the women.

On the 14th October he wrote again, saying that he was in good health and that Paris was a paradise which made him feel twenty years old. Four letters followed; in the first, dated from Paris on S. Martin's Day, he told Francesco not to reply for he did not know whether he would prolong his visit nor where he might go. Finding no fortune in Paris, he said he would go and search elsewhere. On the 23rd, he sent one hundred and fifty lires; "a true blessing," to the poor girl who was always short of money.

Between times, Casanova passed eight days at Fontainebleau, where he met "a charming young man of twenty-five," the son of "the young and lovely O'Morphi" who indirectly owed to him her position, in 1752, as the mistress of Louis XV. "I wrote my name on his tablets and begged him to present my compliments to his mother."

He also met, in the same place, his own son by Mme. Dubois, his former housekeeper at Soleure who had married the good M. Lebel.

"We shall hear of the young gentleman in twenty-one years at Fontainebleau."

"When I paid my third visit to Paris, with the intention of ending my days in that capital, I reckoned on the friendship of M. d'Alembert, but he died, like, Fontenelle, a fortnight after my arrival, toward the end of 1783."

It is interesting to know that, at this time, Casanova met his famous contemporary, Benjamin Franklin. "A few days after the death of the illustrious d'Alembert," Casanova assisted, at the old Louvre, in a session of the Academie des Inscriptions et Belles-Lettres. "Seated beside the learned Franklin, I was a little surprised to hear Condorcet ask him if he believed that one could give various directions to an air balloon. This was the response: 'The matter is still in its infancy, so we must wait.' I was surprised. It is not believable that the great philosopher could ignore the fact that it would be impossible to give the machine any other direction than that governed by the air which fills it, but these people 'nil tam verentur, quam ne dubitare aliqua de re videantur.'"

On the 13th November, Casanova left Paris in company with his brother, Francesco, whose wife did not accompany him. "His new wife drove him away from Paris."

"Now [1797 or 1798] I feel that I have seen Paris and France for the last time. That popular effervescence [the French Revolution] has disgusted me and I am too old to hope to see the end of it."

VIENNA

On the 29th November, Casanova wrote from Frankfort that a drunken postilion had upset him and in the fall he had dislocated his left shoulder, but that a good bone-setter had restored it to place. On the 1st December he wrote that he was healed, having taken medicine and having been blooded. He promised to send Francesca eight sequins to pay her rent. He reached Vienna about the 7th of December and on the 15th sent Francesco a bill of exchange for eight sequins and two lires.

On the last day of 1783, Francesca wrote to him at Vienna:

"I see by your good letter that you will go to Dresden and then to Berlin and that you will return to Vienna the 10th January . . . . I am astonished, my dear friend, at the great journeys you make in this cold weather, but, still, you are a great man, big-hearted, full of spirit and courage; you travel in this terrible cold as though it were nothing . . . . "

On the 9th January, Casanova wrote from Dessau to his brother Giovanni, proposing to make peace with him, but without results. On the 27th, he was at Prague. By the 16th February, he was again in Vienna, after a trip lasting sixty-two days. His health was perfect, and he had gained flesh due, as he wrote Francesca, to his contented mind which was no longer tormented.

In February, he entered the service of M. Foscarini, Venetian Ambassador, "to write dispatches."

On the 10th March, Francesca wrote:

"Dearest of Friends, I reply at once to your good letter of the 28th February which I received Sunday . . . . I thank you for your kindness which makes you say that you love me and that when you have money you will send me some . . . but that at the moment you are dry as a salamander. I do not know what sort of animal that is. But as for me I am certainly dry of money and I am consumed with the hope of having some . . . . I see that you were amused at the Carnival and that you were four times at the masked ball, where there were two hundred women, and that you danced minuets and quadrilles to the great astonishment of the ambassador Foscarini who told everyone that you were sixty years old, although in reality you have not yet reached your sixtieth year. You might well laugh at that and say that he must be blind to have such an idea.

"I see that you assisted, with your brother, at a grand dinner at the Ambassador's . . . .

"You say that you have read my letters to your brother and that he salutes me. Make him my best compliments and thank him. You ask me to advise you whether, if he should happen to return to Venice with you, he could lodge with you in your house. Tell him yes, because the chickens are always in the loft and make no dirt; and, as for the dogs, one watches to see that they do not make dirt. The furniture of the apartment is already in place; it lacks only a wardrobe and the little bed which you bought for your nephew and the mirror; as for the rest, everything is as you left it. . . ."

It is possible that, at the "grand dinner," Casanova was presented to Count Waldstein, without whose kindness to Casanova the Memoirs probably would never have been written. The Lord of Dux, Joseph Charles Emmanuel Waldstein-Wartenberg, Chamberlain to Her Imperial Majesty, descendant of the great Wallenstein, was the elder of the eleven children of Emmanuel Philibert, Count Waldstein, and Maria Theresa, Princess Liechtenstein. Very egotistic and willful in his youth, careless of his affairs, and an imprudent gambler, at thirty years of age he had not yet settled down. His mother was disconsolated that her son could not separate himself from occupations "so little suited to his spirit and his birth."

On the 13th March 1784, Count Lamberg wrote Casanova: "I know M. le C. de Waldstein through having heard him praised by judges worthy of appreciating the transcendent qualities of more than one kind peculiar to the Count. I congratulate you on having such a Maecenas, and I congratulate him in his turn on having chosen such a man as yourself." Which last remark certainly foreshadows the library at Dux.

Later, on the lath March, 1785, Zaguri wrote: "In two months at the latest, all will be settled. I am very happy." Referring further, it is conjectured, to Casanova's hopes of placing himself with the Count.

IV

LETTERS FROM FRANCESCA

20th March 1784. "I see that you will print one of your books; you say that you will send me two hundred copies which I can sell at thirty sous each; that you will tell Zaguri and that he will advise those who wish copies to apply to me . . ."

This book was the Lettre historico-critique sur un fait connu dependant d'une cause peu connue, adressee au duc de * * *, 1784.

3rd April 1784. "I see with pleasure that you have gone to amuse yourself in company with two ladies and that you have traveled five posts to see the Emperor [Joseph II] . . . . You say that your fortune consists of one sequin . . . . I hope that you obtained permission to print your book, that you will send me the two hundred copies, and that I may be able to sell them. . . ."

14th April 1784. "You say that a man without money is the image of death, that he is a very wretched animal. I learn with regret that I am unlikely to see you at the approaching Festival of the Ascension . . . that you hope to see me once more before dying . . . . You make me laugh, telling me that at Vienna a balloon was made which arose in the air with six persons and that it might be that you would go up also."

28th April 1784. "I see, to my lively regret, that you have been in bed with your usual ailment [hemorrhoids]. But I am pleased to know that you are better. You certainly should go to the baths . . . .

I have been discouraged in seeing that you have not come to Venice because you have no money .... P. S. Just at this moment I have received a good letter, enclosing a bill of exchange, which I will go and have paid . . . ."

5th May 1784. "I went to the house of M. Francesco Manenti, at S. Polo di Campo, with my bill of exchange, and he gave me at once eighteen pieces of ten lires each . . . . I figure that you made fun of me saying seriously that you will go up in a balloon and that, if the wind is favorable, you will go in the air to Trieste and then from Trieste to Venice."

19th May 1784. "I see, to my great regret, that you are in poor health and still short of money .... You say that you need twenty sequins and that you have only twenty trari . . . . I hope that your book is printed. . . ."

29th May 1784. "I note with pleasure that you are going to take the baths; but I regret that this treatment enfeebles and depresses you. It reassures me that you do not fail in your appetite nor your sleep.... I hope I will not hear you say again that you are disgusted with everything, and no longer in love with life . . . . I see that for you, at this moment, fortune sleeps . . . . I am not surprised that everything is so dear in the city where you are, for at Venice also one pays dearly and everything is priced beyond reach."

Zaguri wrote Casanova the 12th May, that he had met Francesca in the Mongolfieri casino. And on the 2nd June Casanova, doubtless feeling his helplessness in the matter of money, and the insufficiency of his occasional remittances, and suspicious of

Francesca's loyalty, wrote her a letter of renunciation. Then came her news of the sale of his books; and eighteen months passed before he wrote to her again.

On the 12th June 1784, Francesca replied: "I could not expect to convey to you, nor could you figure, the sorrow that tries me in seeing that you will not occupy yourself any more with me . . . . I hid from you that I had been with that woman who lived with us, with her companion, the cashier of the Academie des Mongolfceristes. Although I went to this Academy with prudence and dignity, I did not want to write you for fear you would scold me. That is the only reason, and hereafter you may be certain of my sincerity and frankness. . . . I beg you to forgive me this time, if I write you something I have never written for fear that you would be angry with me because I had not told you. Know then that four months ago, your books which were on the mezzanine were sold to a library for the sum of fifty lires, when we were in urgent need. It was my mother who did it. . . ."

26th June 1784. ". . . Mme. Zenobia [de Monti] has asked me if I would enjoy her company. Certain that you would consent I have allowed her to come and live with me. She has sympathy for me and has always loved me.."

7th July 1784. "Your silence greatly disturbs me! To receive no more of your letters! By good post I have sent you three letters, with this one, and you have not replied to any of them. Certainly, you have reason for being offended at me, because I hid from you something which you learned from another . . . . But you might have seen, from my last letter, that I have written you all the truth about my fault and that I have asked your pardon for not writing it before.... Without you and your help, God knows what will become of us.... For the rent of your chamber Mme. Zenobia will give us eight lires a month and five lires for preparing her meals. But what can one do with thirteen lires! . . . I am afflicted and mortified. . . . Do not abandon me."

V

LAST DAYS AT VIENNA

In 1785, at Vienna, Casanova ran across Costa, his former secretary who, in 1761, had fled from him taking "diamonds, watches, snuffbox, linen, rich suits and a hundred louis." "In 1785, I found this runagate at Vienna. He was then Count Erdich's man, and when we come to that period, the reader shall hear what I did."

Casanova did not reach this period, in writing his Memoirs, but an account of this meeting is given by Da Ponte, who was present at it, in his Memoirs. Costa had met with many misfortunes, as he told Casanova, and had himself been defrauded. Casanova threatened to have him hanged, but according to Da Ponte, was dissuaded from this by counter accusations made by Costa.

Da Ponte's narration of the incident is brilliant and amusing, in spite of our feeling that it is maliciously exaggerated: "Strolling one morning in the Graben with Casanova, I suddenly saw him knit his brows, squawk, grind his teeth, twist himself, raise his hands skyward, and, snatching himself away from me, throw himself on a man whom I seemed to know, shouting with a very loud voice: 'Murderer, I have caught thee.' A crowd having gathered as a result of this strange act and yell, I approached them with some disgust; nevertheless, I caught Casanova's hand and almost by force I separated him from the fray. He then told me the story, with desperate motions and gestures, and said that his antagonist was Gioachino Costa, by whom he had been betrayed.

This Gioachino Costa, although he had been forced to become a servant by his vices and bad practices, and was at that very time servant to a Viennese gentleman, was more or less of a poet. He was, in fact, one of those who had honored me with their satire, when the Emperor Joseph selected me as poet of his theater. Costa entered a cafe, and while I continued to walk with Casanova, wrote and send him by a messenger, the following verses:

> "'Casanova, make no outcry;
> You stole, indeed, as well as I;
> You were the one who first taught me;
> Your art I mastered thoroughly.
> Silence your wisest course will be.'

"These verses had the desired effect. After a brief silence, Casanova laughed and then said softly in my ear: 'The rogue is right.' He went into the cafe and motioned to Costa to come out; they began to walk together calmly, as if nothing had happened, and they parted shaking hands repeatedly and seemingly calm and friendly. Casanova returned to me with a cameo on his little finger, which by a strange coincidence, represented Mercury, the god-protector of thieves. This was his greatest valuable, and it was all that was left of the immense booty, but represented the character of the two restored friends, perfectly."

Da Ponte precedes this account with a libellous narrative of Casanova's relations with the Marquise d'Urfe, even stating that Casanova stole from her the jewels stolen in turn by Costa, but, as M. Maynial remarks, we may attribute this perverted account "solely to the rancour and antipathy of the narrator." It is more likely that Casanova frightened Costa almost out of his wits, was grimly amused at his misfortunes, and let him go, since there was no remedy to Casanova's benefit, for his former rascality. Casanova's own brief, anticipatory account is given in his Memoirs.

In 1797, correcting and revising his Memoirs, Casanova wrote: "Twelve years ago, if it had not been for my guardian angel, I would have foolishly married, at Vienna, a young, thoughtless girl, with whom I had fallen in love." In which connection, his remark is interesting: "I have loved women even to madness, but I have always loved liberty better; and whenever I have been in danger of losing it, fate has come to my rescue."

While an identification of the "young, thoughtless girl" has been impossible, M. Rava believes her to be "C. M.," the subject of a poem found at Dux, written in duplicate, in Italian and French, and headed "Giacomo Casanova, in love, to C. M."

"When, Catton, to your sight is shown the love Which all my tenderest caresses prove, Feeling all pleasure's sharpest joys and fears, Burning one moment, shivering the next, Caressing you while showering you with tears, Giving each charm a thousand eager kisses, Wishing to touch at once a thousand blisses And, at the ones beyond my power, vexed, Abandoned in a furious desire, Leaving these charms for other charms that fire, Possessing all and yet desiring Until, destroyed by excesses of pleasure, Finding no words of love nor anything To express my fires overflowing measure Than deepening sighs and obscure murmuring: Ah! Then you think to read my inmost heart To find the love that can these signs impart ....Be not deceived. These transports, amorous cries, These kisses, tears, desires and heavy sighs, Of all the fire which devours me Could less than even the lightest tokens be."

Evidently this same girl is the authoress of the two following letters written by "Caton M ...." to Casanova in 1786.

12th April 1786. "You will infinitely oblige me if you will tell me to whom you wrote such pretty things about me; apparently it is the Abbe Da Ponte; but I would go to his house and, either he would prove that you had written it or I would have the honor of telling him that he is the most infamous traducer in the world. I think that the lovely picture which you make of my future has not as much excuse as you may think, and, in spite of your science, you deceive yourself.... But just now I will inform you of all my wooers and you can judge for yourself by this whether I deserve all the reproaches you made me in your last letter. It is two years since I came to know the Count de K . . . ; I could have loved him but I was too honest to be willing to satisfy his desires . . . . Some months afterward, I came to know the Count de M . . . ; he was not so handsome as K . . . , but he possessed every possible art for seducing a girl; I did everything for him, but I never loved him as much as his friend. In fine, to tell you all my giddinesses in a few words, I set everything right again with K . . . . and got myself into a quarrel with M . . . ., then I left K . . . . and returned to M . . . ., but at the house of the latter there was always an officer who pleased me more than both the two others and who sometimes conducted me to the house; then we found ourselves at the house of a friend, and it is of this same officer that I am ill. So, my dear friend, that is all. I do not seek to justify my past conduct; on the contrary, I know well that I have acted badly.... I am much afflicted at being the cause of your remaining away from Venice during the Carnival . . . . I hope to see you soon again and am, with much love,

"Monsieur, your sincere

"Caton M. . . ."

16th July 1786. "I have spoken with the Abbe Da Ponte. He invited me to come to his house because, he said, he had something to tell me for you. I went there, but was received so coldly that I am resolved not to go there again. Also, Mlle. Nanette affected an air of reserve and took at on herself to read me lessons on what she was pleased to call my libertinism . . . . I beg that you will write nothing more about me to these two very dangerous personages.... Just now I will tell you of a little trick which I played on you, which without doubt deserves some punishment. The young, little Kasper, whom you formerly loved, came to ask me for the address of her dear Monsieur de Casanova, so that she could write a very tender letter full of recollections. I had too much politeness to wish to refuse a pretty girl, who was once the favorite of my lover, so just a request, so I gave her the address she wished; but I addressed the letter to a city far from you. Is it not, my dear friend, that you would like well to know the name of the city, so that you could secure the letter by posts. But you can depend on my word that you will not know it until you have written me a very long letter begging me very humbly to indicate the place where the divine letter of the adorable object of your vows has gone. You might well make this sacrifice for a girl in whom the Emperor [Joseph II] interests himself, for it is known that, since your departure from Vienna, it is he who is teaching her French and music; and apparently he takes the trouble of instructing her himself, for she often goes to his house to thank him for his kindnesses to her, but I know not in what way she expresses herself.

"Farewell, my dear friend. Think sometimes of me and believe that I am your sincere friend."

On the 23rd April 1785, the ambassador Foscarini died, depriving Casanova of a protector, probably leaving him without much money, and not in the best of health. He applied for the position of secretary to Count Fabris, his former friend, whose name had been changed from Tognolo, but without success. Casanova then determined to go to Berlin in the hope of a place in the Academy. On the 30th July he arrived at Bruen in Moravia, where his friend Maximilian-Joseph, Count Lamberg gave him, among other letters of recommendation, a letter addressed to Jean-Ferdinand Opiz, Inspector of Finances and Banks at Czaslau, in which he wrote:

"A celebrated man, M. Casanova, will deliver to you, my dear friend, the visiting card with which he is charged for Mme. Opiz and yourself. Knowing this amiable and remarkable man, will mark an epoch in your life, be polite and friendly to him, 'quod ipsi facies in mei memoriam faciatis'. Keep yourself well, write to me, and if you can direct him to some honest man at Carlsbad, fail not to do so. . . ."

On the 15th August 1785, M. Opiz wrote Count Lamberg about Casanova's visit:

"Your letter of the 30th, including your cards for my wife and myself, was delivered the first of this month by M. Casanova. He was very anxious to meet the Princess Lubomirski again at Carlsbad. But as something about his carriage was broken, he was obliged to stop in Czaslau for two hours which he passed in my company. He has left Czaslau with the promise of giving me a day on his return. I am already delighted. Even in the short space of time in which I enjoyed his company, I found in him a man worthy of our highest consideration and of our love, a benevolent philosopher whose homeland is the great expanse of our planet (and not Venice alone) and who values only the men in the kings . . . . I know absolutely no one at Carlsbad, so I sincerely regret being unable to recommend him to anyone there, according to your desire. He did not wish, on account of his haste, to pause even at Prague and, consequently, to deliver, at this time, your letter to Prince Furstemberg."

PART THE THIRD DUX 1786-1798

I

THE CASTLE AT DUX

It is uncertain how long Casanova remained at Carlsbad. While there, however, he met again the Polish nobleman Zawoiski, with whom he had gambled in Venice in 1746. "As to Zawoiski, I did not tell him the story until I met him in Carlsbad old and deaf, forty years later." He did not return to Czaslau, but in September 1785 he was at Teplitz where he found Count Waldstein whom he accompanied to his castle at Dux.

From this time onward he remained almost constantly at the castle where he was placed in charge of the Count's library and given a pension of one thousand florins annually.

Describing his visit to the castle in 1899, Arthur Symons writes: "I had the sensation of an enormous building: all Bohemian castles are big, but this one was like a royal palace. Set there in the midst of the town, after the Bohemian fashion, it opens at the back upon great gardens, as if it were in the midst of the country. I walked through room after room, corridor after corridor; everywhere there were pictures, everywhere portraits of Wallenstein, and battle scenes in which he led on his troops. The library, which was formed, or at least arranged, by Casanova, and which remains as he left it, contains some twenty-five thousand volumes, some of them of considerable value . . . . The library forms part of the Museum, which occupies a ground-floor wing of the castle. The first room is an armoury, in which all kinds of arms are arranged, in a decorative way, covering the ceiling and the walls with strange patterns. The second room contains pottery, collected by Casanova's Waldstein on his Eastern travels. The third room is full of curious mechanical toys, and cabinets, and carvings in ivory. Finally, we come to the library, contained in the two innermost rooms. The book shelves are painted white and reach to the low vaulted ceilings, which are whitewashed. At the end of a bookcase, in the corner of one of the windows, hangs a fine engraved portrait of Casanova."

In this elaborate setting, Casanova found the refuge he so sadly needed for his last years. The evil days of Venice and Vienna, and the problems and makeshifts of mere existence, were left behind. And for this refuge he paid the world with his Memoirs.

II

LETTERS FROM FRANCESCA

In 1786, Casanova renewed his correspondence with Francesca, who wrote:

1st July 1786. "After a silence of a year and a half, I received from you yesterday a good letter which has consoled me in informing me that you are in perfect health. But, on the other hand, I was much pained to see that in your letter you did not call me Friend, but Madame . . . . You have reason to chide me and to reproach me for having rented a house without surety or means of paying the rent. As to the advice you give me that if some honest person would pay me my rent, or at least a part of it, I should have no scruples about taking it because a little more, or a little less, would be of little importance . . . . I declare to you that I have been disconsolated at receiving from you such a reproach which is absolutely unjustified . . . . You tell me that you have near you a young girl who merits all your solicitations and your love, she and her family of six persons who adore you and give you every attention; that she costs you all you have, so that you cannot send me even a sou . . . . I am pained to hear you say that you will never return to Venice, and yet I hope to see you again. . . ."

The "young girl" referred to in Francesca's letter was Anna-Dorothea Kleer, daughter of the porter of the castle. This young girl became pregnant in 1786 and Casanova was accused of seducing her. The guilty one, however, was a painter named Schottner who married the unfortunate girl in January 1787.

9th August 1786.

"My only true friend,

"It is two days since I received your dear letter; I was very happy to see your writing …. You have reason to mortify me and reproach me in recalling all the troubles I caused you, and especially that which you call treachery, the sale of your books, of which in part I was not guilty . . . . Forgive me, my dear friend, me and my foolish mother who, despite all my objections, absolutely insisted on selling them. Regarding that which you write me that you know that my mother, last year, told about that you had been my ruin, this may unhappily be true, since you already know the evil thoughts of my mother, who even says that you are still at Venice . . . . When have I not been always sincere with you, and when have I not at least listened to your good advices and offers? I am in a desperate situation, abandoned by all, almost in the streets, almost about to be homeless . . . . Where are all the pleasures which formerly you procured me? Where are the theatres, the comedies which we once saw together? . . ."

5th January 1787.

"The first of the year I received your dear letter with the bill of exchange for one hundred and twenty-five lires which you sent me so generously . . . . You say you have forgiven me for all the troubles I have caused you. Forget all, then, and do not accuse me any more of things which are but too true and of which the remembrance alone cuts me to the heart . . . . You write me that you have been forgotten by a person of whom you were very fond, that she is married and that you have not seen her for more than a month."

The "person" referred to was Anna Kleer.

5th October 1787.

. . . . "Until the other day, I had been waiting for your arrival, hoping that you would come to assist at the entry of the Procurator Memmo . . . . I see by your good letter that you were not able to get away, since your presence is nearly always necessary in the great castle . . . . I learn of the visit you have received from the Emperor who wished to see your library of forty-thousand volumes! . . . You say that you detest the chase and that you are unhappy when politeness obliges you to go . . . . I am pleased to know that you are in good health, that you are stout and that you have a good appetite and sleep well . . . . I hope that the printing of your book [Histoire de ma fuite] is going according to your wishes. If you go to Dresden for the marriage of your niece, enjoy yourself for me . . . . Forget not to write to me; this gives me such pleasure! Remember me. Full of confidence in your friendship, I am, and always will be, your true and sincere friend,

"Francesca Buschina."

CORRESPONDENCE AND ACTIVITIES

In 1787, a book was published under the title of 'Dreissig Brief uber Galizien by Traunpaur', which included this passage: "The most famous adventurers of two sorts (there are two, in fact: honest adventurers and adventurers of doubtful reputation) have appeared on the scene of the kingdom of Poland. The best known on the shores of the Vistula are: the miraculous Cagliostro: Boisson de Quency, grand charlatan, soldier of fortune, decorated with many orders, member of numerous Academies: the Venetian Casanova of Saint-Gall, a true savant, who fought a duel with Count Branicki: the Baron de Poellnitz . . . the lucky Count Tomatis, who knew so well how to correct fortune, and many others."

In June 1789, Casanova received a letter from Teresa Boisson de Quency, the wife of the adventurer above referred to:

"Much honored Monsieur Giacomo:

"For a long time I have felt a very particular desire to evidence to you the estimation due your spirit and your eminent qualities: the superb sonnet augmented my wish. But the inconveniences of childbirth and the cares required by a little girl whom I adore, made me defer this pleasure. During my husband's absence, your last and much honored letter came to my hands. Your amiable compliments to me, engage me to take the pen to give you renewed assurance that you have in me a sincere admirer of your great talent . . . . When I wish to point out a person who writes and thinks with excellence, I name Monsieur Casanova . . . ."

In 1793, Teresa de Quency wished to return to Venice at which time Zaguri wrote Casanova: "The Bassani has received letters from her husband which tell her nothing more than that he is alive."

Casanova passed the months of May, June and July 1788 at Prague, supervising the printing of the Histoire de ma fuite.

"I remember laughing very heartily at Prague, six years ago, on learning that some thin-skinned ladies, on reading my flight from The Leads, which was published at that date, took great offense at the above account, which they thought I should have done well to leave out."

In May he was troubled with an attack of the grippe. In October, he was in Dresden, apparently with his brother. Around this time "The Magdalene," a painting by Correggio, was stolen from the Museum of the Elector.

On the 30th October 1788, Casanova wrote to the Prince Belozelski, Russian Minister to the Court of Dresden: "Tuesday morning, after having embraced my dear brother, I got into a carriage to return here. At the barrier on the outskirts of Dresden, I was obliged to descend, and six men carried the two chests of my carriage, my two night-bags and my capelire into a little chamber on the ground level, demanded my keys, and examined everything . . . . The youngest of these infamous executors of such an order told me they were searching for 'The Magdalene! . . . The

oldest had the impudence to put his hands on my waistcoat . . . .
At last they let me go.

"This, my prince, delayed me so that I could not reach Petervalden by daylight. I stopped at an evil tavern where, dying of famine and rage, I ate everything I saw; and, wishing to drink and not liking beer, I gulped down some beverage which my host told me was good and which did not seem unpleasant. He told me that it was Pilnitz Moste. This beverage aroused a rebellion in my guts. I passed the night tormented by a continual diarrhoea. I arrived here the day before yesterday (the 28th), where I found an unpleasant duty awaiting me. Two months ago, I brought a woman here to cook, needing her while the Count is away; as soon as she arrived, I gave her a room and I went to Leipzig. On returning here, I found three servants in the hands of surgeons and all three blame my cook for putting them in such a state. The Count's courier had already told me, at Leipzig, that she had crippled him. Yesterday the Count arrived and would do nothing but laugh, but I have sent her back and exhorted her to imitate the Magdalene. The amusing part is that she is old, ugly and ill-smelling."

In 1789, 1791 and 1792, Casanova received three letters from Maddalena Allegranti, the niece of J. B. Allegranti the innkeeper with whom Casanova lodged at Florence in 1771. "This young person, still a child, was so pretty, so gracious, with such spirit and such charms, that she incessantly distracted me. Sometimes she would come into my chamber to wish me good-morning . . . . Her appearance, her grace, the sound of her voice . . . were more than I could resist; and, fearing the seduction would excuse mine,

I could find no other expedient than to take flight. . . . Some years later, Maddalena became a celebrated musician."

At this period of Casanova's life, we hear again of the hussy who so upset Casanova during his visit to London that he was actually on the point of committing suicide through sheer desperation. On the 20th September 1789, he wrote to the Princess Clari, sister of the Prince de Ligne: "I am struck by a woman at first sight, she completely ravishes me, and I am perhaps lost, for she may be a Charpillon."

There were, among the papers at Dux, two letters from Marianne Charpillon, and a manuscript outlining the story of Casanova's relations with her and her family, as detailed in the Memoirs: With the story in mind, the letters from this girl, "the mistress, now of one, now of another," are of interest:

"I know not, Monsieur, whether you forgot the engagement Saturday last; as for me, I remember that you consented to give us the pleasure of having you at dinner to-day, Monday, the 12th of the month. I would greatly like to know whether your ill-humor has left you; this would please me. Farewell, in awaiting the honor of seeing you.

"Marianne de Charpillon."

"Monsieur,

"As I have a part in all which concerns you, I am greatly put out to know of the new illness which incommodes you; I hope that this will be so trifling that we will have the pleasure of seeing you well and at our house, to-day or to-morrow.

"And, in truth, the gift which you sent me is so pretty that I know not how to express to you the pleasure it has given me and how much I value it; and I cannot see why you must always provoke me by telling me that it is my fault that you are filled with bile, while I am as innocent as a new-born babe and would wish you so gentle and patient that your blood would become a true clarified syrup; this will come to you if you follow my advice. I am, Monsieur,

"Your very humble servant,

"[Marianne Charpillon]

"Wednesday at six o'clock"

On the 8th April, 1790, Zaguri wrote in reference to vertigo of which Casanova complained: "Have you tried riding horseback? Do you not think that is an excellent preservative? I tried it this last summer and I find myself very well."

In 1790, Casanova had a conversation with the Emperor Joseph II at
Luxemburg, on the subject of purchased nobility, which he reports in the
Memoirs.

This same year, attending the coronation of Leopold at Prague, Casanova met his grandson (and, probably, as he himself believed, his own son), the son of Leonilda, who was the daughter of Casanova and Donna Lucrezia, and who was married to the Marquis C . . . . In 1792, Leonilda wrote, inviting Casanova to "spend the remainder of my days with her."

In February 1791, Casanova wrote to Countess Lamberg: "I have in my capitularies more than four hundred sentences which pass for aphorisms and which include all the tricks which place one word for another. One can read in Livy that Hannibal overcame the Alps by means of vinegar. No elephant ever uttered such a stupidity. Livy? Not at all. Livy was not a beast; it is you who are, foolish instructor of credulous youth! Livy did not say aceto which means vinegar, but aceta which means axe."

In April 1791, Casanova wrote to Carlo Grimani at Venice, stating that he felt he had committed a great fault in publishing his libel, 'Ne amori ne donne', and very humbly begging his pardon. Also that his Memoirs would be composed of six volumes in octavo with a seventh supplementary volume containing codicils.

In June, Casanova composed for the theater of Princess Clari, at Teplitz, a piece entitled: 'Le Polemoscope ou la Calomnie demasquee par la presence d'esprit, tragicomedie en trois actes'. The manuscript was preserved at Dux, together with another form of the same, having the sub-title of 'La Lorgnette Menteuse ou la Calomnie demasquee'. It may be assumed that the staging of this piece was an occasion of pleasant activity for Casanova.

In January 1792, during Count Waldstein's absence in London or Paris, Casanova was embroiled with M. Faulkircher, maitre d'hotel, over the unpleasant matter indicated in two of Casanova's letters to this functionary:

"Your rascally Vidierol . . . tore my portrait out of one of my books, scrawled my name on it, with the epithet which you taught him and then stuck it on the door of the privy ....

"Determined to make sure of the punishment of your infamous valet, and wishing at the same time to give proof of my respect for Count Waldstein, not forgetting that, as a last resort, I have the right to invade his jurisdiction, I took an advocate, wrote my complaint and had it translated into German . . . . Having heard of this at Teplitz, and having known that I would not save your name, you came to my chamber to beg me to write whatever I wished but not to name you because it would place you wrong before the War Council and expose you to the loss of your pension . . . . I have torn up my first complaint and have written a second in Latin, which an advocate of Bilin has translated for me and which I have deposited at the office of the judiciary at Dux...."

Following this matter, Casanova attended the Carnival at Oberleutensdorf, and left at Dux a manuscript headed 'Passe temps de Jacques Casanova de Seingalt pour le carnaval de l'an 1792 dans le bourg d'Oberleutensdorf'. While in that city, meditating on the Faulkircher incident, he wrote also 'Les quinze pardons, monologue nocturne du bibliothecaire', also preserved in manuscript at Dux, in which we read:

"Gerron, having served twenty years as a simple soldier, acquired a great knowledge of military discipline. This man was not yet seventy years old. He had come to believe, partly from practice, partly from theory, that twenty blows with a baton on the rump are not dishonoring. When the honest soldier was unfortunate enough to deserve them, he accepted them with resignation. The pain was sharp, but not lasting; it did not deprive him of either appetite nor honor . . . . Gerron, becoming a corporal, had obtained no idea of any kind of sorrow other than that coming from the blows of a baton on the rump . . . . On this idea, he thought that the soul of an honest man was no different than a soldier's breech. If Gerron caused trouble to the spirit of a man of honor, he thought that this spirit, like his own, had only a rump, and that any trouble he caused would pass likewise. He deceived himself. The breech of the spirit of an honest man is different than the breech of the spirit of a Gerron who rendered compatible the rank of a military officer with the vile employments of a domestic and the stable-master of some particular lord. Since Gerron deceived himself, we must pardon him all his faults . . ." etc.

Casanova complained of the Faulkircher incident to the mother of Count Waldstein, who wrote: "I pity you, Monsieur, for being obliged to live among such people and in such evil company, but my son will not forget that which he owes to himself and I am sure he will give you all the satisfaction you wish." Also to his friend Zaguri, who wrote, the 16th March: "I hope that the gout in your hand will not torment you any more. . . . You have told me the story I asked about and which begins: 'Two months have passed since an officer, who is at Vienna, insulted me!' I cannot understand whether he who wrote you an insulting letter is at Vienna or whether he is at Dux. When will the Count return? . . .

You should await his return because you would have, among other reasons to present to him, that of not wishing to have recourse to other jurisdiction than his. . . You say your letters have been intercepted? Someone has put your portrait in the privy? The devil! It is a miracle that you have not killed someone. Positively, I am curious to know the results and I hope that you make no mistakes in this affair which appears to me very delicate."

In August 1792, or thereabouts, Da Ponte on his way to Dresden, visited Casanova at Dux, in the hope of collecting an old debt, but gave up this hope on realizing Casanova's limited resources. In the winter of 1792-3 Da Ponte found himself in great distress in Holland. "Casanova was the only man to whom I could apply," he writes in his Memoirs. "To better dispose him, I thought to write him in verse, depicting my troubles and begging him to send me some money on account of that which he still owed me. Far from considering my request, he contented himself with replying, in vulgar prose, by a laconic billet which I transcribe: 'When Cicero wrote to his friends, he avoided telling them of his affairs.'"

In May 1793, Da Ponte wrote from London: "Count Waldstein has lived a very obscure life in London, badly lodged, badly dressed, badly served, always in cabarets, cafes, with porters, with rascals, with . . . we will leave out the rest. He has the heart of an angel and an excellent character, but not so good a head as ours."

Toward the end of 1792, Cssanova wrote a letter to Robespierre, which, as he advises M. Opiz, the 13th January 1793, occupied one hundred and twenty folio pages. This letter was not to be found at Dux and it may possibly have been sent, or may have been destroyed by Casanova on the advice of Abbe O'Kelly. Casanova's feelings were very bitter over the trial of Louis XVI., and in his letters to M. Opiz he complained bitterly of the Jacobins and predicted the ruin of France. Certainly, to Casanova, the French Revolution represented the complete overthrow of many of his cherished illusions.

On the 1st August 1793, Wilhelmina Rietz, Countess Lichtenau (called the Pompadour of Frederic-William II., King of Prussia) wrote to the librarian at Dux:

"Monsieur

"It seems impossible to know where Count Valstaine [Waldstein] is staying, whether he is in Europe, Africa, America, or possibly the Megamiques. If he is there, you are the only one who could insure his receiving the enclosed letter.

"For my part, I have not yet had time to read their history, but the first reading I do will assuredly be that.

"Mademoiselle Chappuis has the honor of recalling herself to your memory, and I have that of being your very humble servant,

"Wilhelmina Rietz."

The allusions to a "history" and to the 'Megamiques' in this letter refer to Casanova's romance, 'Icosameron'.

About this time, Count Waldstein returned to Dux after having been, at Paris, according to Da Ponte, concerned in planning the flight of Louis XVI., and in attempting to save the Princess Lamballe. On the 17th August, Casanova replied to the above letter:

"Madame,

"I handed the Count your letter two minutes after having received it, finding him easily. I told him that he should respond at once, for the post was ready to go; but, as he begged to wait for the following ordinary, I did not insist. The day before yesterday, he begged me to wait again, but he did not find me so complaisant. I respond to you, Madame, for his carelessness in replying to letters is extreme; he is so shameful that he is in despair when he is obliged to it. Although he may not respond, be sure of seeing him at your house at Berlin after the Leipzig Fair, with a hundred bad excuses which you will laugh at and pretend to believe good ones . . . . This last month, my wish to see Berlin again has become immeasurable, and I will do my best to have Count Waldstein take me there in the month of October or at least to permit me to go . . . . You have given me an idea of Berlin far different than that the city left with me when I passed four months there twenty-nine years ago . . . . If my 'Icosameron' interests you, I offer you its Spirit. I wrote it here two years ago and I would not have published it if I had not dared hope that the Theological Censor would permit it. At Berlin no one raised the least difficulty . . . . If circumstances do not permit me to pay you my respects at Berlin, I hope for the happiness of seeing you here next year . . . ."

Sometime after this and following his quarrel with M. Opiz, Casanova evidently passed through a period of depression, as indicated by a manuscript at Dux, headed "Short reflection of a philosopher who finds himself thinking of procuring his own death," and dated "the 13th December 1793, the day dedicated to S. Lucie, remarkable in my too long life."

"Life is a burden to me. What is the metaphysical being who prevents me from slaying myself? It is Nature. What is the other being who enjoins me to lighten the burdens of that life which brings me only feeble pleasures and heavy pains? It is Reason. Nature is a coward which, demanding only conservation, orders me to sacrifice all to its existence. Reason is a being which gives me resemblance to God, which treads instinct under foot and which teaches me to choose the best way after having well considered the reasons. It demonstrates to me that I am a man in imposing silence on the Nature which opposes that action which alone could remedy all my ills.

"Reason convinces me that the power I have of slaying myself is a privilege given me by God, by which I perceive that I am superior to all animals created in the world; for there is no animal who can slay itself nor think of slaying itself, except the scorpion, which poisons itself, but only when the fire which surrounds it convinces it that it cannot save itself from being burned. This animal slays itself because it fears fire more than death. Reason tells me imperiously that I have the right to slay myself, with the divine oracle of Cen: 'Qui non potest vivere bene non vivat male.' These eight words have such power that it is impossible that a man to whom life is a burden could do other than slay himself on first hearing them."

Certainly, however, Casanova did not deceive himself with these sophisms, and Nature, who for many years had unquestionably lavished her gifts on him, had her way.

Over the end of the year, the two mathematicians, Casanova and Opiz, at the request of Count Waldstein, made a scientific examination of the reform of the calendar as decreed the 5th October 1793 by the National Convention.

In January 1795, Casanova wrote to the Princess Lobkowitz to thank her for her gift of a little dog. On the 16th the Princess wrote from Vienna:

"Monsieur,

"I am enchanted at the charming reception you accorded the dog which I sent you when I learned of the death of your well-loved greyhound, knowing that she would nowhere be better cared for than with you, Monsieur. I hope with all my heart that she has all the qualities which may, in some fashion, help you to forget the deceased . . . ."

In the autumn of 1795, Casanova left Dux. The Prince de Ligne writes in his Memoirs: "God directed him to leave Dux. Scarcely believing in more than his death, which he no longer doubted, he pretended that each thing he had done was by the direction of God and this was his guide. God directed him to ask me for letters of recommendation to the Duke of Weimar, who was my good friend, to the Duchess of Gotha, who did not know me, and to the Jews of Berlin. And he departed secretly, leaving for Count Waldstein a letter at once tender, proud, honest and irritating. Waldstein laughed and said he would return. Casanova waited in ante-chambers; no one would place him either as governor, librarian or chamberlain. He said everywhere that the Germans were thorough beasts. The excellent and very amiable Duke of Weimer welcomed him wonderfully; but in an instant he became jealous of Goethe and Wieland, who were under the Duke's protection. He declaimed against them and against the literature of the country which he did not, and could not, know. At Berlin, he declaimed against the ignorance, the superstition and the knavery of the Hebrews to whom I had addressed him, drawing meanwhile, for the money they claimed of him, bills of exchange on the Count who laughed, paid, and embraced him when he returned. Casanova laughed, wept, and told him that God had ordered him to make this trip of six weeks, to leave without speaking of it, and to return to his chamber at Dux. Enchanted at seeing us again, he agreeably related to us all the misfortunes which had tried him and to which his susceptibility gave the name of humiliations. 'I am proud,' he said, 'because I am nothing'. . . . Eight days after his return, what new troubles! Everyone had been served strawberries before him, and none remained for him."

The Prince de Ligne, although he was Casanova's sincere friend and admirer, gives a rather somber picture of Casanova's life at Dux: "It must not be imagined that he was satisfied to live quietly in the refuge provided him through the kindness of Waldstein. That was not within his nature. Not a day passed without trouble; something was certain to be wrong with the coffee, the milk, the dish of macaroni, which he required each day. There were always quarrels in the house. The cook had ruined his polenta; the coachman had given him a bad driver to bring him to see me; the dogs had barked all night; there had been more guests than usual and he had found it necessary to eat at a side table. Some hunting-horn had tormented his ear with its blasts; the priest had been trying to convert him; Count Waldstein had not anticipated his morning greeting; the servant had delayed with his wine; he had not been introduced to some distinguished personage who had come to see the lance which had pierced the side of the great Wallenstein; the Count had lent a book without telling him; a groom had not touched his hat to him; his German speech had been misunderstood; he had become angry and people had laughed at him."

Like Count Waldstein, however, the Prince de Ligne made the widest allowances, understanding the chafing of Casanova's restless spirit. "Casanova has a mind without an equal, from which each word is extraordinary and each thought a book."

On the 16th December, he wrote Casanova: "One is never old with your heart, your genius and your stomach."

Casanova's own comment on his trip away from Dux will be found in the Memoirs. "Two years ago, I set out for Hamburg, but my good genius made me return to Dux. What had I to do at Hamburg?"

On the 10th December, Casanova's brother Giovanni [Jean] died. He was the Director of the Academy of Painting at Dresden. Apparently the two brothers could not remain friends.

Giovanni left two daughters, Teresa and Augusta, and two sons, Carlo and Lorenzo. While he was unable to remain friendly with his brother, Casanova apparently wished to be of assistance to his nieces, who were not in the best of circumstances, and he exchanged a number of letters with Teresa after her father's death.

On the occasion of Teresa Casanova's visit to Vienna in 1792, Princess Clari, oldest sister of the Prince de Ligne, wrote of her: "She is charming in every way, pretty as love, always amiable; she has had great success. Prince Kaunitz loves her to the point of madness."

In a letter of the 25th April 1796, Teresa assured her "very amiable and very dear uncle" that the cautions, which occupied three-fourths of his letter, were unnecessary; and compared him with his brother Francois, to the injury of the latter. On the 5th May, Teresa wrote:

"Before thanking you for your charming letter, my very kind uncle, I should announce the issue of our pension of one hundred and sixty crowns a year, which is to say, eighty crowns apiece; I am well satisfied for I did not hope to receive so much." In the same letter, Teresa spoke of seeing much of a "charming man," Don Antonio, who was no other than the rascally adventurer Don Antonio della Croce with whom Casanova had been acquainted since 1753, who assisted Casanova in losing a thousand sequins at Milan in 1763; who in 1767, at Spa, following financial reverses, abandoned his pregnant mistress to the charge of Casanova; and who in August 1795, wrote to Casanova: "Your letter gave me great pleasure as the sweet souvenir of our old friendship, unique and faithful over a period of fifty years."

It is probable that, at this time, Casanova visited Dresden and Berlin also. In his letter "To Leonard Snetlage," he writes: "'That which proves that revolution should arrive,' a profound thinker said to me in Berlin, last year, 'is that it has arrived.'"

On the 1st March, 1798, Carlo Angiolini, the son of Maria Maddalena, Casanova's sister, wrote to Casanova: "This evening, Teresa will marry M. le Chambellan de Veisnicht [Von Wessenig] whom you know well." This desirable marriage received the approval of Francesco also. Teresa, as the Baroness Wessenig, occupied a prominent social position at Dresden. She died in 1842.

Between the 13th February and the 6th December 1796, Casanova engaged in a correspondence with Mlle. Henriette de Schuckmann who was visiting at Bayreuth. This Henriette (unfortunately not the Henriette of the Memoirs whose "forty letters" to Casanova apparently have not been located), had visited the library at Dux in the summer of 1786. "I was with the Chamberlain Freiberg, and I was greatly moved, as much by your conversation as by your kindness which provided me with a beautiful edition of Metastasio, elegantly bound in red morocco." Finding herself at Bayreuth in an enforced idleness and wishing a stimulant, wishing also to borrow some books, she wrote Casanova, under the auspices of Count Koenig, a mutual friend, the 13th February 1796, recalling herself to his memory. Casanova responded to her overtures and five of her letters were preserved at Dux. On the 28th May Henriette wrote:

"But certainly, my good friend, your letters have given me the greatest pleasure, and it is with a rising satisfaction that I pore over all you say to me. I love, I esteem, I cherish, your frankness . . . . I understand you perfectly and I love to distraction the lively and energetic manner with which you express yourself."

On the 30th September, she wrote: "You will read to-day, if you please, a weary letter; for your silence, Monsieur, has given me humors. A promise is a debt, and in your last letter you promised to write me at least a dozen pages. I have every right to call you a bad debtor; I could summon you before a court of justice; but all these acts of vengeance would not repair the loss which I have endured through my hope and my fruitless waiting . . . . It is your punishment to read this trivial page; but although my head is empty, my heart is not so, and it holds for you a very living friendship."

In March 1797, this Henriette went to Lausanne and in May from there to her father's home at Mecklenburg.

CORRESPONDENCE WITH JEAN-FERDINAND OPIZ

On the 27th July 1792, Casanova wrote M. Opiz that he had
finished the twelfth volume of his Memoirs, with his age at forty-
seven years 1772. "Our late friend, the worthy Count Max Josef
Lamberg," he added, "could not bear the idea of my burning my
Memoirs, and expecting to survive me, had persuaded me to send
him the first four volumes. But now there is no longer any
questions that his good soul has left his organs. Three weeks ago I
wept for his death, all the more so as he would still be living if he
had listened to me. I am, perhaps, the only one who knows the
truth. He who slew him was the surgeon Feuchter at Cremsir, who
applied thirty-six mercurial plasters on a gland in his left groin
which was swollen but not by the pox, as I am sure by the
description he gave me of the cause of the swelling. The mercury
mounted to his esophagus and, being able to swallow neither
solids nor fluids, he died the 23rd June of positive famine . . . . The
interest of the bungling surgeon is to say that he died of the pox.
This is not true, I beg, you to give the lie to anyone you hear
saying it. I have before my eyes four hundred and sixty of his
letters over which I weep and which I will burn. I have asked Count
Leopold to burn mine, which he had saved, and I hope that he will
please me by doing it. I have survived all my true friends.
'Tempus abire mihi est' Horace says to me.

"Returning to my Memoirs . . . I am a detestable man; but I do not
care about having it known, and I do not aspire to the honor of the
detestation of posterity. My work is full of excellent moral

instructions. But to what good, if the charming descriptions of my offences excite the readers more to action than to repentance? Furthermore, knowing readers would divine the names of all the women and of the men which I have masked, whose transgressions are unknown to the world, my indiscretion would injure them, they would cry out against my perfidy, even though every word of my history were true . . . . Tell me yourself whether or not I should burn my work? I am curious to have your advice."

On the 6th May 1793, Casanova wrote Opiz: "The letter of recommendation you ask of me to the professor my brother for your younger son, honors me; and there is no doubt that, having for you all the estimation your qualities merit, I should send it to you immediately. But this cannot be. And here is the reason. My brother is my enemy; he has given me sure indications of it and it appears that his hate will not cease until I no longer exist. I hope that he may long survive me and be happy. This desire is my only apology."

"The epigraph of the little work which I would give to the public," Casanova wrote the 23rd August 1793, "is 'In pondere et mensura'. It is concerned with gravity and measure. I would demonstrate not only that the course of the stars is irregular but also that it is susceptible only to approximate measures and that consequently we must join physical and moral calculations in establishing celestial movements. For I prove that all fixed axes must have a necessarily irregular movement of oscillation, from which comes a variation in all the necessary curves of the planets which compose their eccentricities and their orbits. I demonstrate that light has neither body nor spirit; I demonstrate that it comes in an instant from its respective star; I demonstrate the impossibility of many parallaxes and the uselessness of many others. I criticize not only Tiko-Brahi, but also Kepler and Newton . . . .

"I wish to send you my manuscript and give you the trouble of publishing it with my name at Prague or elsewhere . . . . I will sell it to the printer or to yourself for fifty florins and twenty-five copies on fine paper when it is printed."

But Opiz replied:

"As the father of a family, I do not feel myself authorized to dispose of my revenues on the impulse of my fancy or as my heart suggests.... and no offer of yours could make me a book-seller."

This shows plainly enough that Opiz, for all his interest in Casanova, had not the qualities of true friendship.

On the 6th September 1793, Casanova wrote:

"I will have my Reveries printed at Dresden, and I will be pleased to send you a copy. I laughed a little at your fear that I would take offense because you did not want my manuscript by sending me the ridiculous sum I named to you. This refusal, my dear friend, did not offend me. On the contrary it was useful as an aid in knowing character. Add to this that in making the offer I thought to make you a gift. Fear nothing from the event. Your system of economy will never interfere with either my proceedings or my doctrines; and I am in no need of begging you, for I think that your action followed only your inclination and consequently your greatest pleasure."

On the insistence of Opiz, Casanova continued his correspondence, but he passed over nothing more, neither in exact quotations from Latin authors, nor solecisms, nor lame reasonings. He even reproached him for his poor writing and did not cease joking at the philanthropic and amiable sentiments Opiz loved to parade while at the same time keeping his purse-strings tight. A number of quarreling letters followed, after which the correspondence came to an end. One of Casanova's last letters, that of the 2nd February 1794, concludes: "One day M. de Bragadin said to me: 'Jacques, be careful never to convince a quibbler, for he will become your enemy.' After this wise advice I avoided syllogism, which tended toward conviction. But in spite of this you have become my enemy. . . ."

Among the Casanova manuscripts at Dux was one giving his final comment on his relations with Opiz. Accusing Opiz of bringing about a quarrel, Casanova nevertheless admits that he himself may not be blameless, but lays this to his carelessness. "I have a bad habit," he writes, "of not reading over my letters. If, in re-reading those I wrote to M. Opiz, I had found them bitter, I would have burned them." Probably Casanova struck the root of the matter in his remark, "Perfect accord is the first charm of a reciprocal friendship." The two men were primarily of so different a temperament, that they apparently could not long agree even on subjects on which they were most in accord.

The complete correspondence is of very considerable interest.

V

PUBLICATIONS

In 1786, Casanova published 'Le soliloque d'un penseur', in which he speaks of Saint-Germain and of Cagliostro. On the 23rd December 1792, Zaguri wrote Casanova that Cagliostro was in prison at San Leo. "Twenty years ago, I told Cagliostro not to set his foot in Rome, and if he had followed this advice he would not have died miserably in a Roman prison."

In January 1788, appeared 'Icosameron' a romance in five volumes, dedicated to Count Waldstein, which he describes as "translated from the English." This fanciful romance, which included philosophic and theological discussions, was the original work of Casanova and not a translation. It was criticized in 1789 by a literary journal at Jena. Preserved at Dux were several manuscripts with variants of 'Icosameron' and also an unpublished reply to the criticism.

In 1788 Casanova published the history of his famous flight from "The Leads". An article on this book appeared in the German 'Litteratur-Zeitung', 29th June 1789: "As soon as the history was published and while it was exciting much interest among us and among our neighbors, it was seen that other attempts at flight from prisons would make their appearance. The subject in itself is captivating; all prisoners awake our compassion, particularly when they are enclosed in a severe prison and are possibly innocent . . . . The history with which we are concerned has all the appearances of truth; many Venetians have testified to it, and the principal character, M. Casanova, brother of the celebrated painter, actually lives at Dux in Bohemia where the Count Waldstein has established him as guardian of his important library."

In July 1789 there was discovered, among the papers of the Bastille, the letter which Casanova wrote from Augsburg in May 1767 to Prince Charles of Courlande on the subject of fabricating gold. Carrel published this letter at once in the third volume of his 'Memoirs authentiques et historiques sur la Bastille'. Casanova kept a copy of this letter and includes it in the Memoirs.

In October 1789, Casanova wrote M. Opiz that he was writing to a professor of mathematics [M. Lagrange] at Paris, a long letter in Italian, on the duplication of the cube, which he wished to publish. In August 1790, Casanova published his 'Solution du Probleme Deliaque demontree and Deux corollaires a la duplication de hexadre'. On the subject of his pretended solution of this problem in speculative mathematics, Casanova engaged with M. Opiz in a heated technical discussion between the 16th September and 1st November 1790. Casanova sought vainly to convince Opiz of the correctness of his solution. Finally, M. Opiz, tired of the polemics, announced that he was leaving on a six-weeks tour of inspection and that he would not be able to occupy himself with the duplication of the cube for some time to come. On the 1st November, Casanova wished him a pleasant journey and advised him to guard against the cold because "health is the soul of life."

In 1797, appeared the last book published during Casanova's lifetime, a small work entitled: 'A Leonard Snetlage, docteur en droit de l'Universite de Goettingue, Jacques Casanova, docteur en droit de l'Université de Padoue'. This was a careful criticism of the neologisms introduced into French by the Revolution. In reference to Casanova's title of "Doctor," researches by M. Favoro at the University of Padua had failed to establish this claim, although, in the Memoirs Casanova had written:

"I remained at Padua long enough to prepare myself for the Doctor's degree, which I intended to take the following year." With this devil of a man, it is always prudent to look twice before peremptorily questioning the truth of his statement. And in fact, the record of Casanova's matriculation was discovered by Signor Bruno Brunelli.

VI

SUMMARY of MY LIFE

The 2nd November, 1797, Cecilia Roggendorff wrote to Casanova: "By the way, how do you call yourself, by your baptismal name? On what day and in what year were you born? You may laugh, if you wish, at my questions, but I command you to satisfy me . . ." To this request, Casanova responded with:

"Summary of My Life:—my mother brought me into the world at Venice on the 2nd April, Easter day of the year 1725. She had, the night before, a strong desire for crawfish. I am very fond of them.

"At baptism, I was named Jacques-Jerome. I was an idiot until I was eight-and-a-half years old. After having had a hemorrhage for three months, I was taken to Padua, where, cured of my imbecility, I applied myself to study and, at the age of sixteen years I was made a doctor and given the habit of a priest so that I might go seek my fortune at Rome.

"At Rome, the daughter of my French instructor was the cause of my being dismissed by my patron, Cardinal Aquaviva.

"At the age of eighteen years, I entered the military service of my country, and I went to Constantinople. Two years afterward, having returned to Venice, I left the profession of honor and, taking the bit in my teeth, embraced the wretched profession of a violinist. I horrified my friends, but this did not last for very long.

"At the age of twenty-one years, one of the highest nobles of Venice adopted me as his son, and, having become rich, I went to see Italy, France, Germany and Vienna where I knew Count Roggendorff. I returned to Venice, where, two years later, the State Inquisitors of Venice, for just and wise reasons, imprisoned me under The Leads.

"This was the state prison, from which no one had ever escaped, but, with the aid of God, I took flight at the end of fifteen months and went to Paris. In two years, my affairs prospered so well that I became worth a million, but, all the same, I went bankrupt. I made money in Holland; suffered misfortune in Stuttgart; was received with honors in Switzerland; visited M. de Voltaire; adventured in Genoa, Marseilles, Florence and in Rome where the Pope Rezzonico, a Venetian, made me a Chevalier of Saint-Jean-Latran and an apostolic protonotary. This was in the year 1760.

"In the same year I found good fortune at Naples; at Florence I carried off a girl; and, the following year, I was to attend the Congress at Augsburg, charged with a commission from the King of Portugal. The Congress did not meet there and, after the publication of peace, I passed on into England, which great misfortunes caused me to leave in the following year, 1764. I avoided the gibbet which, however, should not have dishonored me as I should only have been hung. In the same year I searched in vain for fortune at Berlin and at Petersburg, but I found it at Warsaw in the following year. Nine months afterwards, I lost it through being embroiled in a pistol duel with General Branicki; I pierced his abdomen but in eight months he was well again and I was very much pleased. He was a brave man. Obliged to leave Poland, I returned to Paris in 1767, but a 'lettre de cachet' obliged me to leave and I went to Spain where I met with great misfortunes. I committed the crime of making nocturnal visits to the mistress of the 'vice-roi', who was a great scoundrel.

"At the frontiers of Spain, I escaped from assassins only to suffer, at Aix, in Provence, an illness which took me to the edge of the grave, after spitting blood for eighteen months.

"In the year 1769, I published my Defense of the Government of Venice, in three large volumes, written against Amelot de la Houssaie.

"In the following year the English Minister at the Court of Turin sent me, well recommended, to Leghorn. I wished to go to Constantinople with the Russian fleet, but as Admiral Orlof, would not meet my conditions, I retraced my steps and went to Rome under the pontificate of Ganganelli.

"A happy love affair made me leave Rome and go to Naples and, three months later, an unhappy love made me return to Rome. I had measured swords for the third time with Count Medini who died four years ago at London, in prison for his debts.

"Having considerable money, I went to Florence, where, during the Christmas Festival, the Archduke Leopold, the Emperor who died four or five years ago, ordered me to leave his dominions within three days. I had a mistress who, by my advice, became Marquise de * * * at Bologna.

"Weary of running about Europe, I determined to solicit mercy from the
Venetian State Inquisitors. For this purpose, I established myself at
Trieste where, two years later, I obtained it. This was the 14th
September 1774. My return to Venice after nineteen years was the most
pleasant moment of my life.

"In 1782, I became embroiled with the entire body of the Venetian
nobility. At the beginning of 1783, I voluntarily left the
ungrateful country and went to Vienna. Six months later I went
to Paris with the intention of establishing myself there, but my
brother, who had lived there for twenty-six years, made me forget
my interests in favor of his. I rescued him from the hands of his
wife and took him to Vienna where Prince Kaunitz engaged him
to establish himself. He is still there, older than I am by two years.

"I placed myself in the service of M. Foscarini, Venetian
Ambassador, to write dispatches. Two years later, he died in my
arms, killed by the gout which mounted into his chest. I then set
out for Berlin in the hope of securing a position with the Academy,
but, half way there, Count Waldstein stopped me at Teplitz and
led me to Dux where I still am and where, according to all
appearances, I shall die.

"This is the only summary of my life that I have written, and I
permit any use of it which may be desired.

"'Non erubesco evangelium'.

"This 17th November 1797.

"Jacques Casanova."

In reference to Casanova's ironic remark about his escape from England, see his conversation, on the subject of "dishonor," with Sir Augustus Hervey at London in 1763, which is given in the Memoirs.

VII

LAST DAYS AT DUX

Scattered through the Memoirs are many of Casanova's thoughts about his old age. Some were possibly incorporated in the original text, others possibly added when he revised the text in 1797. These vary from resignation to bitterness, doubtless depending on Casanova's state of mind at the moment he wrote them:

"Now that I am seventy-two years old, I believe myself no longer susceptible of such follies. But alas! that is the very thing which causes me to be miserable."

"I hate old age which offers only what I already know, unless I should take up a gazette."

"Age has calmed my passions by rendering them powerless, but my heart has not grown old and my memory has kept all the freshness of youth."

"No, I have not forgotten her [Henriette]; for even now, when my head is covered with white hair, the recollection of her is still a source of happiness for my heart."

"A scene which, even now, excites my mirth."

"Age, that cruel and unavoidable disease, compels me to be in good health, in spite of myself."

"Now that I am but the shadow of the once brilliant Casanova, I love to chatter."

"Now that age has whitened my hair and deadened the ardor of my senses, my imagination does not take such a high flight and I think differently."

"What embitters my old age is that, having a heart as warm as ever, I have no longer the strength necessary to secure a single day as blissful as those which I owed to this charming girl."

"When I recall these events, I grow young again and feel once more the delights of youth, despite the long years which separate me from that happy time."

"Now that I am getting into my dotage, I look on the dark side of everything. I am invited to a wedding and see naught but gloom; and, witnessing the coronation of Leopold II, at Prague, I say to myself, 'Nolo coronari'. Cursed old age, thou art only worthy of dwelling in hell."

"The longer I live, the more interest I take in my papers. They are the treasure which attaches me to life and makes death more hateful still."

And so on, through the Memoirs, Casanova supplies his own picture, knowing very well that the end, even of his cherished memories, is not far distant.

In 1797, Casanova relates an amusing, but irritating incident, which resulted in the loss of the first three chapters of the second volume of the Memoirs through the carelessness of a servant girl at Dux who took the papers "old, written upon, covered with scribbling and erasures," for "her own purposes," thus necessitating a re-writing, "which I must now abridge," of these chapters. Thirty years before, Casanova would doubtless have made love to the girl and all would have been forgiven. But, alas for the "hateful old age" permitting no relief except irritation and impotent anger.

On the 1st August, 1797, Cecilia Roggendorff, the daughter of the Count Roggendorff [printed Roquendorf] whom Casanova had met at Vienna in 1753, wrote: "You tell me in one of your letters that, at your death, you will leave me, by your will, your Memoirs which occupy twelve volumes."

At this time, Casanova was revising, or had completed his revision of, the twelve volumes. In July 1792, as mentioned above, Casanova wrote Opiz that he had arrived at the twelfth volume. In the Memoirs themselves we read, ". . . the various adventures which, at the age of seventy-two years, impel me to write these Memoirs . . .," written probably during a revision in 1797.

At the beginning of one of the two chapters of the last volume, which were missing until discovered by Arthur Symons at Dux in 1899, we read: "When I left Venice in the year 1783, God ought to have sent me to Rome, or to Naples, or to Sicily, or to Parma, where my old age, according to all appearances, might have been happy. My genius, who is always right, led me to Paris, so that I might see my brother Francois, who had run into debt and who was just then going to the Temple. I do not care whether or not he owes me his regeneration, but I am glad to have effected it. If he had been grateful to me, I should have felt myself paid; it seems to me much better that he should carry the burden of his debt on his shoulders, which from time to time he ought to find heavy. He does not deserve a worse punishment. To-day, in the seventy-third year of my life, my only desire is to live in peace and to be far from any person who might imagine that he has rights over my moral liberty, for it is impossible that any kind of tyranny should not coincide with this imagination."

Early in February, 1798, Casanova was taken sick with a very grave bladder trouble of which he died after suffering for three-and-a-half months. On the 16th February Zaguri wrote: "I note with the greatest sorrow the blow which has afflicted you." On the 31st March, after having consulted with a Prussian doctor, Zaguri sent a box of medicines and he wrote frequently until the end.

On the 20th April Elisa von der Recke, whom Casanova had met, some years before, at the chateau of the Prince de Ligne at Teplitz, having returned to Teplitz, wrote: "Your letter, my friend, has deeply affected me. Although myself ill, the first fair day which permits me to go out will find me at your side." On the 27th, Elisa, still bedridden, wrote that the Count de Montboisier and his wife were looking forward to visiting Casanova. On the 6th May she wrote, regretting that she was unable to send some crawfish soup, but that the rivers were too high for the peasants to secure the crawfish. "The Montboisier family, Milady Clark, my children and myself have all made vows for your recovery." On the 8th, she sent bouillon and madeira.

On the 4th June, 1798, Casanova died. His nephew, Carlo Angiolini was with him at the time. He was buried in the

churchyard of Santa Barbara at Dux. The exact location of his
grave is uncertain, but a tablet, placed against the outside wall of
the church reads:

> JAKOB
> CASANOVA
> Venedig 1725 Dux 1798

The End